THE HORRORS OF COLORS

THE HAUNTED MANSION

A COLORING BOOK FOR ADULTS

 KATE TAYLOR DESIGN 

This book features 40 intricate illustrations. Each illustration is printed on one side of the page, providing a convenient and enjoyable coloring experience for adults.

If you would like to reorder, please scan the QR Code

THE HAUNTED MANSION:

A Coloring Book for Adults" is a hauntingly beautiful coloring book that transports you to a world of haunted mansions and eerie creatures. Perfect for both experienced coloring enthusiasts and those new to the hobby, this book will challenge and captivate you with its very intricate designs and dark themes. Immerse yourself in a world of terror. "The Haunted Mansion: A Coloring Book for Adults" is a must-have for anyone who loves to color and be scared at the same time.

WIABR

KATE TAYLOR DESING

MYSTICAL CREATURES

- A Dragon Coloring Book for Adults
- A Unicorn Coloring Book for Adults
- A Phoenix Coloring Book fo Adults
- A Fairy Coloring Book for Adults
- A Mermaid Coloring Book for Adults
- A Goblin Coloring Book for Adults
- A Gnome Coloring Book for Adults
- A Troll Coloring Book for Adults
- A Gryphon Coloring Book for Adults

VEHICLES

- American muscle cars coloring book for kids
- Supercars coloring book for kids
- Antique car coloring book for kids
- Jumbo cars coloring book for kids
- Motorcycle Coloring book for kids

THE HORRORS OF COLOR

- The Dark Carnival: A Coloring Book for Adult
- The Haunted Mansion: A Coloring Book for Adults
- Horror coloring book

MANDALAS AND PATTERNS

- Geometric shapes and patterns coloring book
- Adult coloring book tessellations patterns
- Adult coloring book geometric patterns
- Adult coloring book circular patterns.
- 150 Mandala coloring book

QUOTES

- Inspirational quotes from the bible coloring book
- Money quotes coloring book
- Quotes for success coloring book
- Funny Mom Quotes and Patterns coloring book
- Motivational swear words coloring book

CHILDREN

- The Toddler Coloring Book
- Unicorn Coloring Book
- Dinosaur Coloring Book
- Mermaid Coloring Book
- Kawaii Friends Coloring Book

OTHER

- Flower coloring book
- Reverse coloring book

Scan the QR Code